artist TRADING card

WORKSHOP

create **COLLECT** SWAP

bernie BERLIN

NORTH LIGHT BOOKS
Cincinnati, Ohio

www.artistsnetwork.com

ABOUT BERNIE

Bernadette Berlin is a nationally known mixed-media artist and owner of Eggsquisite Creations and The Cre8tive Eye Studio. In October of 2003, she originated the Artist Trading Card Yahoo Group, which proudly acts as an ATC trading forum for more than two thousand members. Bernie has taught ATC techniques and workshops at major art retreats such as Artfest and Art Unraveled. An Artist-on-Call for Stampington, her publication contributions include *Somerset Studio, Cloth Paper Scissors, Rubber Stamp Madness, Inspirations* and Stampington's *An Anthology of Artist Trading Cards.* An avid animal lover, Bernie is the owner of A Place to Bark Dog Rescue. Currently residing in Tennessee with her husband, eight dogs, eleven cats and whatever else needs rescuing at the moment, you can visit Bernie at www.picturetrail.com/thecre8tivei or www.aplacetobark.com.

ARTIST TRADING CARD WORKSHOP. Copyright © 2007 by Bernadette Berlin. Manufactured in China. All rights reserved. The patterns and drawings in the book are for the personal use of the reader. By permission of the author and publisher, they may be either hand-traced or photocopied to make single copies, but under no circumstances may they be resold or republished. It is permissible for the purchaser to make the projects contained herein and sell them at fairs, bazaars and craft shows. No other part of this book may be reproduced in any form or by any electronic or mechanical means including information storage and retrieval systems without permission in writing from the publisher, except by a reviewer, who may quote a brief passage in review. Published by North Light Books, an imprint of F+W Publications, Inc., 4700 East Galbraith Road, Cincinnati, Ohio 45236. (800) 289-0963. First edition.

11 10 09 08 07 5 4 3 2 1

Distributed in Canada by Fraser Direct
100 Armstrong Avenue
Georgetown, ON, Canada L7G 5S4
Tel: (905) 877-4411

Distributed in the U.K. and Europe by David & Charles
Brunel House, Newton Abbot, Devon, TQ12 4PU, England
Tel: (+44) 1626 323200, Fax: (+44) 1626 323319
E-mail: postmaster@davidandcharles.co.uk

Distributed in Australia by Capricorn Link
P.O. Box 704, S. Windsor, NSW 2756 Australia
Tel: (02) 4577-3555

Library of Congress Cataloging-in-Publication Data

Berlin, Bernie.
Artist trading card workshop : create - collect - swap / Bernadette Berlin.
    p. cm.
Includes index.
ISBN-13: 978-1-58180-848-3 (pbk. : alk. paper)
ISBN-10: 1-58180-848-8 (pbk. : alk. paper)
1. Miniature craft. 2. Trading cards. I. Title.
TT178.B48 2006
760--dc22

2006016750

fw
F+W PUBLICATIONS, INC.

Editor: Tonia Davenport
Cover Designer: Karla Baker
Designer: Righteous Planet Design, Inc.
Layout Artist: Neal Miles
Production Coordinator: Greg Nock
Photographers: Christine Polomsky and Tim Grondin; Jim Gilmore and Sang Hoon Park, OMS Photo
Photo Stylist: Jan Nickum

METRIC CONVERSION CHART

TO CONVERT	TO	MULTIPLY BY
Inches	Centimeters	2.54
Centimeters	Inches	0.4
Feet	Centimeters	30.5
Centimeters	Feet	0.03
Yards	Meters	0.9
Meters	Yards	1.1
Sq. Inches	Sq. Centimeters	6.45
Sq. Centimeters	Sq. Inches	0.16
Sq. Feet	Sq. Meters	0.09
Sq. Meters	Sq. Feet	10.8
Sq. Yards	Sq. Meters	0.8
Sq. Meters	Sq. Yards	1.2
Pounds	Kilograms	0.45
Kilograms	Pounds	2.2
Ounces	Grams	28.3
Grams	Ounces	0.035

DEDICATION

This book is dedicated to all the artists who create the beauty we call art.

I hope this book inspires those who love art to create art, to embrace every part of the process and to share a part of themselves with the world. In days such as these, goodwill and acts of kindness are so valuable; it is so important to keep sending good intentions and love to others, even perfect strangers. This is where ATCs fit in.

My special dedication is to my mother and the mothers of this world who allow their children to be artists, to smile and encourage them every step of the way.

I am an artist. I am here to live out loud.
—Emile Zola

ACKNOWLEDGMENTS

To my husband, Jeff, you are my biggest supporter in life and love. I thank you for your support, belief and never-ending encouragement in following my dreams. The success of my artistic endeavors and the animals rescued are because you believed in me.

My deepest appreciation and thanks go to the editors and staff at North Light Books for believing in my vision and giving me this chance to share my love of ATCs with others. The North Light family works as a team to help the writer create the best books possible, in a comfortable, stress-free environment (making it a dream for a first-time author).

A special thanks to Tonia Davenport, for your tireless efforts in keeping me organized, focused and on track, which is not the easiest task in my constantly changing and challenging world!

TABLE OF CONTENTS

The top was too high for me to see.

ALWAYS TRADED—
NEVER SOLD

THE ACT OF **SHARING** ARTIST TRADING CARDS
KNOWS NO **GEOGRAPHICAL BOUNDARIES**
AND BRINGS **LIKE SOULS** TOGETHER ON A LEVEL THAT
NO OTHER **FORM OF COMMUNICATION** CAN.

The act of creating and swapping artist trading cards is an exciting way to share your art, connect with other artists and collect art! This book is for all ages and all levels of artistic know-how. Adults, teenagers and small children, experienced or aspiring, can all benefit from this engaging art form.

Artist trading cards, or ATCs, as they are usually referred to, encompass all types of media. As you will see in this book, cards are made from paper, fabric and metal. They feature the work of photographers, print-makers, watercolorists, collage artists, doodlers, metal crafters and many mixed-media enthusiasts. Therein lies the allure, for it's never been easier to build such a diverse collection of art than it is by collecting ATCs.

People across the continents are sharing and trad-ing their art in this form. ATCs make art accessible to those who appreciate art but may not be able to afford it. When you trade an ATC with another person, it is a selfless act of sharing, as you surrender a piece of your-self without the expectation of monetary gain in return. Art for art's sake.

The format for this art form is of a small nature: 2½" × 3½" (6cm × 9cm). You may be able to create many pieces of art in a short period of time. By creat-ing art daily you sharpen your skills, evolve and grow as an artist. The smaller format is wonderful for children as well—to share, gift and store art of their own for future viewing.

Symbolism, imagination, unique statements, passionate emotions—all can be expressed in the cards you will create. This book will not only teach you the ins and outs of ATCs, but it is my hope to inspire you to embrace your art and your life as one. *Artist Trading Card Workshop* will feed the artist's need to create, in an instant-gratification sort of way, as a wide range of applications with informative explana-tions are covered and showcased.

The number-one steadfast rule of ATCs is they should never be sold. Selling diminishes the true sense of sharing and community among artists. Trading is just that—sharing your art with others for no other reason than wanting to gift a piece of your-self to another.

The second rule is one of etiquette—ATCs acquired in trades should also never be sold. The whole experience of ATCs is not to make money but to connect and collect the art of other artists. If you have acquired many cards and would no longer like to keep them, donate them to a museum or art cen-ter or give them to another artist. Regardless of your experience as an artist, after experiencing the social culture that accompanies artist trading cards, you will look at collecting and creating art in a new way.

HiSTORY OF ATCs

Although miniature works of art created on cards have been around for centuries, the modern-day concept of ATCs was conceptualized by artist m. vänci stirnemann in 1996. In May 1997, stirnemann held a gallery showing of 1,200 cards at the INK.art & text bookstore in Zürich, Switzerland, for which he collaborated with artists Cat Schick and Gido Dietrich. Those attending the show were told that if they wanted to acquire a card that was on display they should bring in one of their own creations to trade for it. A movement was then born that denounced the tradition of critiquing and appraising art, and embraced the process of one artist connecting with another.

One attendee of the first trading session in Zürich was Canadian Don Mabie (Chuck Stake). Mabie was so enthused by the concept of artists sharing with one another in this way that he brought the idea home with him to Calgary and held the first North American trading session (in collaboration with m. vänci stirnemann) at The New Gallery in Calgary, Alberta, Canada. The First International Biennial of Artist Trading Cards included eighty artists from ten different countries and took place in September 2000.

Since that first exhibit, regular trading sessions have been held at The New Gallery every month, and a five-year anniversary was celebrated there on September 28, 2002. As many as seventy-five individuals have attended the monthly trading sessions with a core group of thirty to thirty-five in regular attendance. Participants include artists, art students and members of the general public ranging in age from children to senior citizens.

In-person trading sessions quickly spread from The New Gallery across Canada and the United States, and interest continues to spread across the globe. While it is always most conducive to the trading culture to exchange cards in person, there are also multiple opportunities for trading over the Internet through various groups.

For more information on the history and process of Artist Trading Cards, visit the following Web links:

www.artist-trading-cards.ch (the original ATC site)
www.cedarseed.com/air/atc.html
www.atcquarterly.com

For a list of places to find trading sessions online, see Collect + Swap, page 115.

heaven.

create

THE BIGGEST REASON I AM SO ENAMORED BY ARTIST TRADING CARDS is that the artistic possibilities are endless. You can use any media to create your cards as long as you stay true to the size of the cards. Paint, draw, sew, sculpt, scratch, tear, melt . . .

On the following pages you'll encounter numerous technique ideas to apply to your own ATCs. Whether you've made cards before or you're anxiously waiting to enter this new world, I hope you'll have fun exploring all of the possibilities you'll find throughout these pages. There really are no limits to how you choose to express yourself in this trading card format. If you love to draw or doodle—great! Maybe the world of collage is where you're most comfortable—that works! Or, perhaps you've always been known as a sewing sensation—then sew or stitch your cards in the same way you pour passion into an art quilt or an embroidered gift.

Just as with any other art form, if you create cards on a regular basis, you will see your art evolve, and you can't help but want to explore new ground occasionally. That's where *Artist Trading Card Workshop* comes in—let this be your inspiration to try something new or to be reminded of something you enjoyed doing long ago but have since forgotten.

Most importantly, remember that ATCs are meant to be exchanged. Make art to share!

INTUITIVE WATERCOLOR

This intuitive watercolor technique is a fun, childlike way to create art. By just allowing the watercolor to randomly saturate the paper and flow into abstract shapes, we can then use our imaginations to outline the images we see. Opening your mind is a creative exercise in art, allowing yourself to see images; training your eye is part of the process and can help you develop your intuitive talents. If you don't see any definitive shapes or images, no worries—just start doodling. Think about how you feel, about the world around you. . .the shapes and images will come. Use this technique alone for a card or as a background.

What You Will Need

palette paper

watercolor brush

water-soluble oil pastels

watercolor paper

liquid watercolor (or dye ink)

heat gun

fine-point black pen

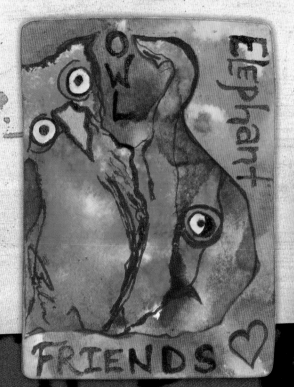

1

2

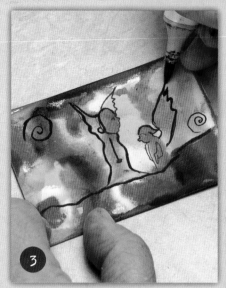

3

Saturate Paper

Working on a piece of palette paper, randomly lay some color down around the edges of the watercolor paper, and with a wet brush, spread out the color over the paper. Make sure there is a good amount of water on the paper.

Add Drops of Color

Next, drop liquid watercolor onto the wet paper and blow it around with a heat gun.

Envision Forms

Add more watercolor if you wish, and repeat with the heat gun. When the paper is dry, look at it and try to envision an image made by the unusual shapes of color, and outline them with a fine-point pen. Here, I am seeing a couple of angelic figures.

Claudine Hellmuth

catch the burning

sparks that fly

Katie Kendrick

WATERCOLOR ON BABY WIPES

Baby wipes are a staple on my work table. I've never been one to throw things away, so they are used not only to clean up but to blend colors and background media. Then they become "fabric" for an ATC. When paints have been applied to the baby wipes they have a strong fabric-like feel to them. In addition to making the most of random paint and ink splotches, a variation is to fold the baby wipe in half, apply ink and unfold. It can be like a Rorschach inkblot test. Have fun! What do you see? You can also cut shapes from them and stitch them onto cards.

What You Will Need

baby wipes
scrap paper
palette paper
liquid watercolors
glue or gel medium
scissors

Jen Osborn

Squirt on Watercolor

Set a clean baby wipe on a piece of scrap paper, then set that on a piece of palette paper and randomly squirt liquid watercolor over the wipe.

Reserve Scrap Paper

The scrap paper that has absorbed the paint can now be used as a background for cards, too! Set both the baby wipe and the scrap paper aside to dry.

beau temps, n'est-ce pas?

Sarah Fishburn

Adhere Baby Wipe to Card and Trim

Apply glue or gel medium to a card and then adhere the card to the wipe. Trim the excess wipe from around the card, using scissors. Note: The baby wipe used here was one that came out of the package with an embossed pattern. You may like incorporating this into your art, or you may wish to use solid, "unquilted" baby wipes.

Izabella Pierce

Paint
ON PAPER TOWEL

Paper towels come in many types and textures. They are easily accessible and inexpensive, and the texture takes to the rich, deep color of metallic paint in wonderful ways. You can collect a variety from many different places (think of all the public restrooms you encounter in a week!). This technique can be used on whole paper towels, on torn pieces or layers of different towels, or even mixed with other papers. While I primarily use this as a background, you may love it so much that you will want to consider it alone on a card.

What You Will Need

brush
paper towel
Lumiere paints, at least
  three colors
gel medium
scissors
rubber stamp
quick-drying
  ink pad

OLD EASTER

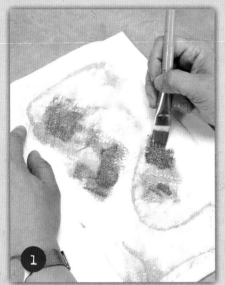

1

Apply Paint to Towel
Using a brush, randomly apply paint to the paper towel. (If you cover the entire towel, you will have enough to make several cards.) Set the paper towel aside to dry.

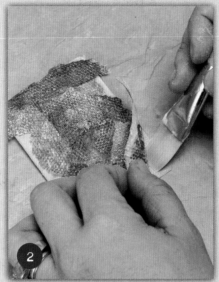

2

Layer Pieces onto Card
Tear the paper towel into pieces and layer on enough pieces to cover the card, using gel medium.

3

Trim Excess Towel
Trim the excess paper towel with scissors. One option you have now is to stamp it with a large stamp and a quick-drying ink.

Céline Navarro

Kim Rae Nugent

Jamie Markle

LEAFING PEN RESIST

Metallic pen is resistant to watercolor or spray inks. By applying your metallic pen first and then adding paint or ink afterward, you can achieve some very dramatic effects. Metallic leafing pens now come in a variety of metal colors, from copper to chrome, and there are a few different tip sizes to choose from, too. These pens also work wonderfully for edging cards to add a special finishing touch.

What You Will Need

watercolor paper
metallic leafing pen
   (Krylon)
brush
liquid watercolor
fluid black acrylic paint
rubber stamp

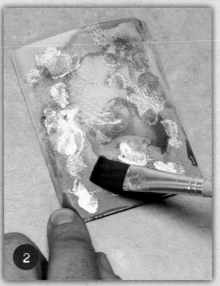

1 Apply Leafing and First Color

This technique works best on watercolor paper. Draw on a card with a metallic leafing pen. Here I am using gold. Then use a brush to apply liquid watercolor over the card. See how the metallic pen resists the watercolor?

2 Apply More Color

Apply a second color, and let the two blend together. Let dry.

3 Stamp with Black Paint

Dab fluid black acrylic paint onto a rubber stamp, and stamp over the dried pen and watercolor.

Nancy Breen

Izabella Pierce

PENNY DANCE
One Dance-One Couple
MAJESTIC HALL
205194

Colette George

iNKY LaYERS

This layering technique came about as a result of me having too many rubber stamping supplies that would just dry up from not being used fast enough. By adding my stamping inks to my paints to create mixed-media collage backgrounds, I've found a way to use up these inks before they dry up. This technique creates many effects that will draw interest to your cards—depth of color, texture and a somewhat distressed look if you use old papers for your collage background. The old papers really soak up paint, glues and gel media.

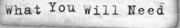

What You Will Need

dye ink pad
colored glazing medium
pigment ink pad
iridescent ink (Luna Lights)

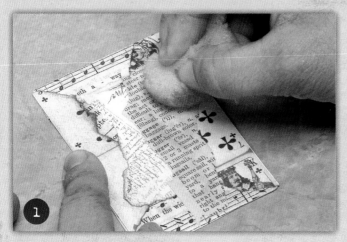

Lay Down Variety of Paper

Make a collage from a variety of old paper and new paper (for a good variety in ink absorption). I like to ink up some of the edges before I collage them down. Using a sponge and a dye ink pad, apply areas of color to the card. Leave some white areas.

Add Colored Glaze

Next, apply a colored glaze over the entire card, and blot up the excess. Yellow is my favorite glazing color.

Dab on Pigment Ink

To apply the pigment ink layer, it's easy to use a direct-to-paper technique with little ink pads, such as ColorBox Cat's Eye. Dab the color on in limited areas. If you apply too much color in any one spot, you can wipe it away with a baby wipe.

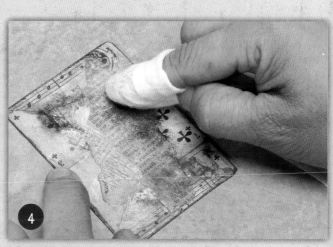

Blend in Iridescent Ink

The last layer to apply is iridescent ink that is semitransparent. I have found Luna Lights to work the best, but you can substitute iridescent calligraphy ink. Drop a tiny bit on the card, then blot the ink with a baby wipe and blend it in.

STENCILS

Stencils are great! Easy to use and available in many shapes and sizes, you can use them minimally as focal images or continue to stencil the same pattern over and over to create a background. Even the stencil itself can be used as an embellishment sometimes.

What You Will Need

- heavy-bodied acrylic paints, mixture of dark and light colors
- stencils, two sizes
- cosmetic sponge

Pounce Through First Stencil

Color a card with an acrylic color of your choice. Place your first stencil on the card and pounce with a dark heavy-bodied acrylic paint and a cosmetic sponge.

Pounce Through Second Stencil

After the paint is dry from the first stencil, choose a second stencil and pounce a white or light-colored acrylic paint through it.

Linda Woods

Mary Haldeman

Sarah Fishburn

MAGaZiNE PaPER

Magazines and catalogs are everywhere. They are works of art unto themselves. By using old magazines, you are both recycling and creating new artwork. I highly recommend that when you use magazine photos you alter them. Cut them up, write over them, paint out imagery and make them look very different from what they originally were. Give them a second life, reincarnated into something they never dreamed they'd be! The words and phrases from magazines are fun to use, too.

What You Will Need

magazine images
scissors
gel medium
small brush
paint
black marker
sponge
dye ink pads
opaque pens

DEFINE eternity?

Split Image

Combine Images for Background

Look for interesting textures on magazine pages and combine several together to form the background of the card.

Create Composition

Layer sections of the magazine paper to cover the card. There may be one image, such as a face, that can be cut into strips for a more interesting effect.

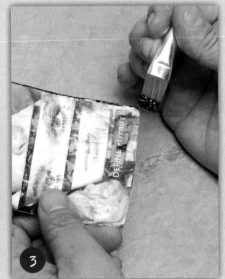

Finish off Edges

After you have layered everything on with gel medium, it's nice to finish off the edges with either paint or a black marker.

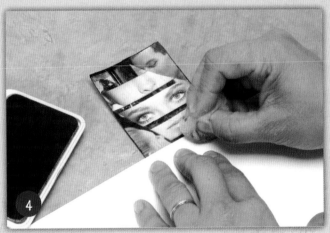

Dab on Color

Using a sponge, add some color from dye ink pads.

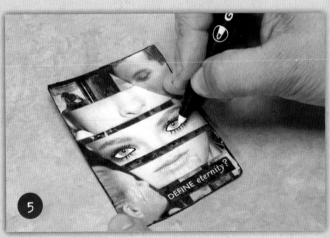

Add Final Details

Add details and highlights to the images with opaque pens. Then seal the entire card with more gel medium.

Izabella Pierce

Anna Barrow-Boekweg

Lyn Cardinal

each song is pre-cious

Katie Kendrick

Izabella Pierce

Field Notes

Reiny Rizzi-Gruhlke

Heather Crossley

Izabella Pierce

Kelly Snelling

Sarah Fishburn

Kelly Snelling

Katie Kendrick

SOUL

they came in a thin continuous stream

Gesso and Magazine Images

This is a wonderful exercise for those who are intimidated by facial studies for painting or drawing. Think of a magazine image as a guide of sorts. By creating a veil of gesso over your picture, you allow yourself to learn the feel of drawing a face. Do this over and over and in time you will be able to draw your own faces without using the "template." You can also use this technique on photocopies of your own personal pictures.

What You Will Need

ATC Wizard Tool, optional
  (European Papers, Ltd)

magazine image

scissors

gel medium

gesso

fine-point permanent black
  marker

opaque markers

acrylic paint

detail
  brush

Find an Image

Use the ATC Wizard Tool to find an image you would like for your card. If you do not have this tool, you can make your own framing device by cutting out an ATC-sized rectangle from a piece of cardstock.

Cut Image Out

Cut the image out and adhere it to the card with gel medium. Using a dry brush and very light pressure, apply gesso over the entire card, using a crosshatch motion. You still want to be able to see the image, but this softens it a bit.

Define Image

Let the gesso dry. Take a fine-point pen or marker and define the area you want to bring out. Add your own details to both the background and the image. Give your figure accessories!

Peter Hollinghurst

Color Image In

Begin coloring with paint and a detail brush in some areas. This is similar to paint-by-numbers. It's okay if you paint over some of the pen lines—you can go back over them later, if you wish. Don't be afraid to try changing things like the shape of the hair or the design in the background.

Add Opaque Pen Details

Finally, tidy up any areas that need redefining with the black pen and embellish the card with opaque markers or paint pens.

Kim Rae Nugent

Angela Cartwright

Maria Lamb

Claudine Hellmuth

Angela Cartwright

Corey Moortgat

A Taste of the Truth.

just throw the bums out,

Jamie Markle

Peter Hollinghurst

NeVR-DULL

This is a technique that I learned in a class with Gail Russakov, and I have been hooked on it ever since! Nevr-Dull is actually a metal polish and cleaner, but along with removing dirt and tarnish from many types of metal, it also does a fine job of removing the toner from magazine pages! One thing I love about this technique is that it's always a bit of a surprise how the piece is going to turn out. Have I gotten your curiosity piqued? Check it out!

What You Will Need

    magazine image
    gel medium
    scissors
    Elmer's Glue-All
    Nevr-Dull
    water-soluble oil pastels
    blending stick (optional)

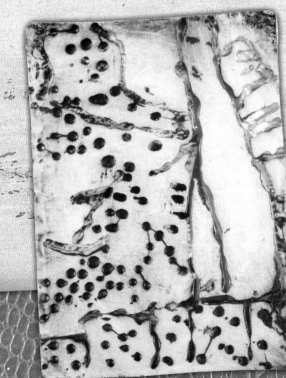

1

Apply Glue in Several Areas

Mount the magazine image to the card using gel medium, and trim away the excess magazine page with scissors. Apply glue along many lines in the magazine image. Set aside to dry.

2

Wipe Away Printing

Take a clump of Nevr-Dull and begin wiping away the magazine color from the card. Where there is glue, the color will remain and act as a resist. You can take away as much or as little as you like.

3

Replace Color with Pastels

Add in some color with the oil pastels and rub it in with your fingers or, if you wish, a blending stick.

Gail Russakov

Gail Russakov

Gail Russakov

PHONE BOOK PAPER

Phone books have always intrigued me. Call me silly, but it's just amazing to see that many names in one place. How fun would it be to send out ATCs randomly to people in the phone book, with a note describing what ATCs are and that there would be no need to reciprocate? Just a gift from a perfect stranger. Phone books are appealing in the sense that they are easy to find. You throw them away each year, and they're free! I like the paper, as it absorbs paints and glues easily. The pages also can be easily layered for depth and texture for the background of collage work.

What You Will Need

phone book pages
gel medium
brayer
scissors
acrylic paint
glazing medium
baby wipes
opaque pen (optional)

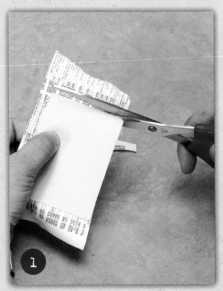

1

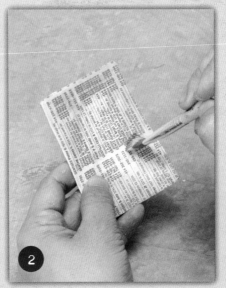

2

3

Glue Card to Page

Glue a card to a page ripped out of the phone book, using gel medium. Brayer the paper down well, then use scissors to cut the card away from the rest of the page.

Add Color

Apply a mixture of acrylic paint and glazing medium to the front of the card, and wipe off the excess with a baby wipe.

Layer Second Color

Apply a second color layer to add some depth. Wipe off in the same manner as the first color.

4

Seal Edges

Add additional glazing mixture to the edges. Dry well. Your background is now complete and you can add whatever collage elements you choose. Here, I stuck clear round stickers over assorted heads from figures in magazines and cut them out. Then I added final details with an opaque pen.

Peter Hollinghurst

Corey Moortgat

Claudine Hellmuth

Reiny Rizzi

Debrina Pratt

Debrina Pratt

Debrina Pratt

STRING

Wind it, tie it, lace it—string is lots of fun! This technique combines string, gesso, paper and paint to make cards with a lot of interesting texture and depth. Substitute rubber bands, yarn or other string-like things. String is inexpensive and adds a great tactile element to your cards.

What You Will Need

mat board for card

string, twine or other
fiber

gesso

gel medium

black-and-white
photocopies

acrylic paint

remember moments

legacy
OF ♥ LOVE

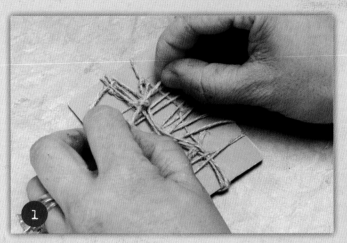

Wrap Card in String

Wrap string around the card several times, in at least a couple of different directions, and secure with one or two knots.

Coat with Gesso

Cover the entire front of the card with gesso.

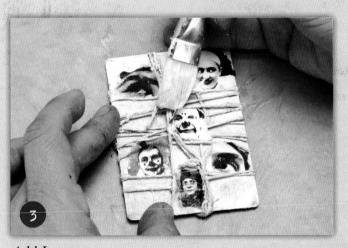

Add Images

Add collage images to the card with gel medium. You should place some of the images over the string.

Apply Layers of Paint

Soften the edges of the paper pieces with a bit of gesso. Now you can paint over the card with washes of color. Pounce with a denser consistency of paint in the string areas to work in the paint. I like to work with about three close-in-value colors at a time.

SUDOKU

Reiny Rizzi

Barbe Saint John

Lyn Cardinal

CHOW MEIN
(Pan Fried Soft Noodles)
$5.25

7. Vegetable Chow Mein........................$5.95
8. Pork Chow Mein..............................$5.95
9. Chicken Chow Mein.........................$5.95
0. Beef Chow Mein..............................$7.50
1. Shrimp

long life

Linda Woods

Peter Hollinghurst

THAT'S MAKE
ENTIRELY THE
TOO WORLD
IT'S BETTER
TIME PLACE
TO

Eunice Timoney Ravenna

eternally present

praise

Katie Kendrick

Aggie

NEW FRIENDS

Jacob

Maria Lamb

TiSSUE PaPER

Tissue paper is very versatile and inexpensive. There are many things you can do with it, such as squish, layer, paint, tear and distress it. I recommend using plain white tissue for this technique. Commercial colored tissue may bleed or alter the colors of your card, and while this may be what you want, consider yourself warned. Colored tissue is not lightfast and will fade or change color with time. If you want color, just add paint. Try embedding small objects into the wet tissue for added interest.

What You Will Need

gift tissue
gel medium
small brush
acrylic paint

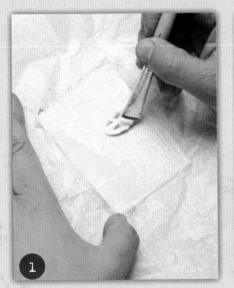

1

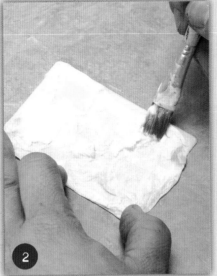

2

3

Adhere First Tissue Layer

Apply a layer of gel medium to the card. Set a piece of tissue over the wet gel medium and gently press to smooth it down.

Add Crumpled Tissue

Apply another coat of gel medium over the top of the tissue, then crumple up the overhanging tissue and press it back onto the card, using more gel medium to secure, as necessary.

Add Paint

Apply paint over the crinkled tissue paper. This can be done while the gel medium is either wet or dry, depending on the effect you want. I like to add the paint while the gel medium is still wet and blend a couple of colors together. (Smooth out any air bubbles with your brush as you work.)

Tonia Davenport

Angela Cartwright

Josie Cirincione

TRANSFERS

Transfers are a great method if you want to feature a particular image on your card. Water or gel medium can be used depending on the effect you are looking for. Transferred photos or artwork can have a distressed, old and worn feel to them. Never one to throw things away, I like to save the used photo paper to use in a future card.

What You Will Need

watercolor paper for card

color ink-jet images on
  lightweight photo paper

water

brush

brayer

gel medium

muslin

Confessions

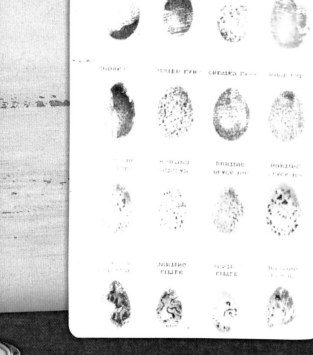

WATER ONTO PAPER

1

Dampen Card
Using a brush, apply water to a watercolor paper card.

2

Burnish Image Facedown
Place the image facedown on the damp paper, and use a brayer over the back of the photo paper.

3

Peel off Photo Paper
Gently peel off the photo paper to reveal the transfer.

GEL MEDIUM ONTO PAPER OR MUSLIN

1

Coat Card with Gel Medium
Apply gel medium to the card with a brush.

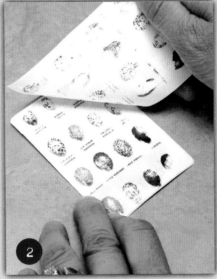

2

Brayer Image over Card
Place the image facedown onto the gel medium and brayer the back. Gently peel off the photo paper.

3

Repeat for Muslin
The process for transferring onto fabric is the same as it is for paper.

Josie Cirincione

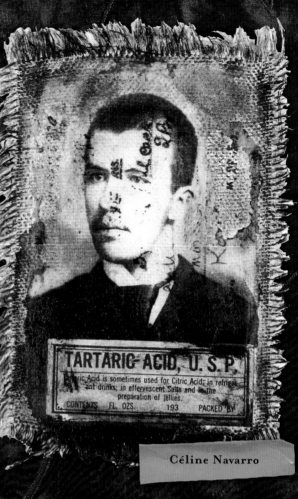

Céline Navarro

Sarah Fishburn

Maria Lamb

Suzette McGrath

Lesley Riley

IRIS HOEY.

create

Diane Glos

Maureen Blackman

FUN FOAM

Fun foam (thin, condensed foam rubber) is sold in craft stores and usually comes with an adhesive back. It is easily cut with scissors and, when combined with acrylic paint, really gives your cards a "fun" dimension!

What You Will Need

- fun foam
- scissors
- gel medium
- brush
- gesso
- acrylic paints
- quick-drying pigment ink
- rubber stamp

merrychristmas

Adhere Shapes to Card

Cut shapes out of fun foam (or use die-cut sticker versions) and adhere them to the card using gel medium.

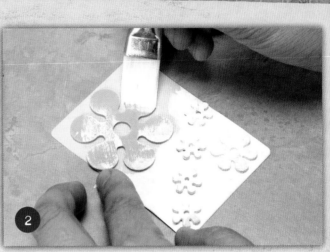

Apply Gesso

Cover the shapes and card with a layer of gesso.

Pounce on Paint

After the gesso has dried, apply acrylic paint over the entire card. I like to use at least two colors. You may need to pounce with the brush, stipple style, to work the paint around the foam shapes.

Add a Stamped Image

Stamp over the card with a large rubber stamp and quick-drying pigment ink. You may wish to stamp it a couple of different times.

Heather Crossley

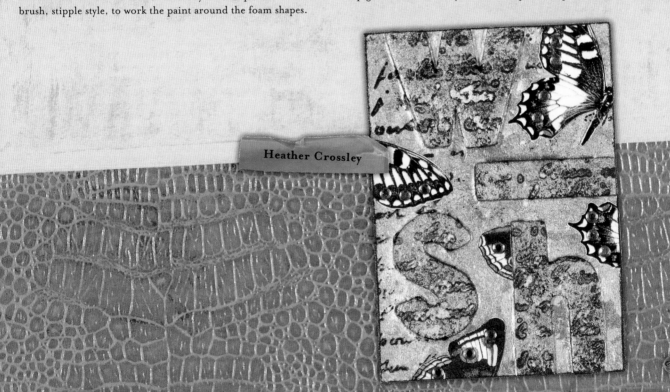

EMBOSS-RESIST

Having fun with embossing powder and an iron can create unexpected depth and an unusual effect. This process is similar to that of using masking fluid with watercolor, though the finished product is often a bit more distressed looking. Sometimes the scrap paper (complete with removed paint) can be used in future cards as well!

What You Will Need

brush
acrylic paint
stamp
clear embossing pad
clear embossing powder
heat gun
scrap paper or cardstock
iron

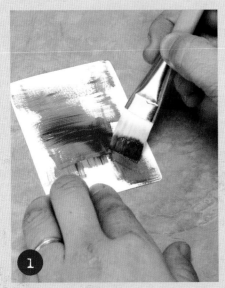

1

2

3

Coat Card with Paint
Cover a card with a layer of acrylic paint. This will be the color that will show through the resist.

Stamp and Add Powder
Add another color if you wish. After the card is dry, stamp an image over the paint, using a clear embossing pad. Sprinkle on enough clear embossing powder to cover the card, and tap off the excess.

Drybrush Contrasting Color
Heat to melt the powder using a heat gun. Drybrush over the embossed card with a contrasting acrylic color. Let dry.

4

5

Apply Hot Iron
Place a scrap of paper over the painted card (be sure you're working on a heat-resistant surface) and apply a hot iron over the paper, using a good amount of pressure.

Peel off Scrap Paper
While it's still warm, peel off the scrap paper. You'll see some of the paint will be removed. This is good! Go over the card again with the iron, using a clean area of the scrap paper. You can repeat this process again to create more depth, or simply collage onto the card now, as it is.

eMBOSSiNG SCRaPS

Everyone has scraps lying around. Instead of throwing them in the trash, create unusual backgrounds with them. This technique provides an effect that's reminiscent of mortar between cracks or of a rich patina that has snuck in cracks and crevices over time. Embossing powder comes in many colors and different textures that, when melted, create the effect of rust, shiny metal, opalescent pearl or sparkly glitter.

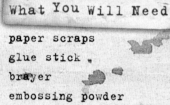

paper scraps
glue stick
brayer
embossing powder
heat gun

6. the season when plants en winter and summer. spring [*spring* flowers].

Sarah Fishburn

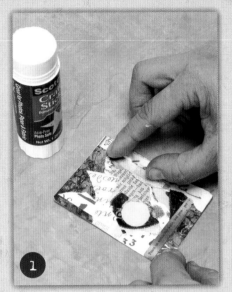

Layer Scraps with Glue Stick

Glue down random scraps of paper using a glue stick. Be liberal with the glue—you want it to ooze out a bit—then brayer the pieces down. I like to use a lot of pieces.

Add Embossing Powder

Cover the card with embossing powder and tap off the excess. (The powder will stick to the gluey edges.)

Melt Powder

Heat the powder to melt with a heat gun.

Mary Haldeman

Sarah Fishburn

Mary Haldeman

ReSIN FReSCO

The effect that I usually get from this technique reminds me of spattered paint but with an added depth of texture. It's fun to layer the powder over different backgrounds and colors to achieve different results. It's also fun just to rub your fingers over the finished card (if you're the tactile type). You can also try this technique without the gesso for more of a wet look, but I like the way the gesso makes the color pop.

What You Will Need

embossing ink pad

ultra-thick embossing
  powder (Ranger)

heat gun

gesso

acrylic paint

brush

Christine Doyle

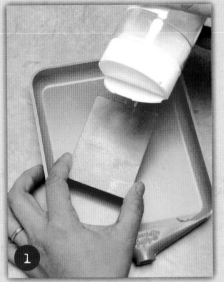

Sprinkle on Embossing Granules

Dab embossing ink onto the card in several random areas. Sprinkle the embossing granules over the ink.

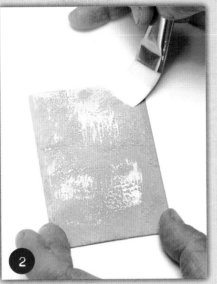

Melt the Granules

Tap off the excess and then heat to melt with a heat gun. Do not overheat it or it will be less textured and more glass-like. Let cool, then brush gesso over the embossed card.

Brush Paint over Embossing

When the gesso dries, drybrush an acrylic paint over the card. Feel free to use more than one color.

Rebecca Zuniga

Gloria Page

GLaSS-LIKe RESIN

You can use this technique to put a finishing touch on a collaged card, or you can apply it to a simple backdrop of acrylic or watercolor. The melted powder makes the color behind it appear glass-like and vibrant, and if you stamp into it, the stamped impression leaves a dull softness that is the perfect contrast. I like to use a stamp that's large enough to cover the entire card, but smaller images or phrases would work just as well. The resin can be cracked once it has cooled for a dramatic broken effect.

What You Will Need

brush
acrylic paint
clear embossing ink pad
ultra-thick embossing
  powder (Ranger)
heat gun
large rubber stamp

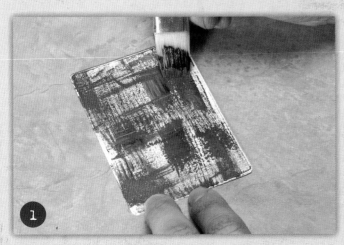

Drybrush Two Colors

Drybrush one color of paint onto the card, using vertical strokes, then drybrush a second color over the first, using horizontal strokes.

Coat Card with One Layer of Powder

Dab clear embossing ink over the entire surface of the card. Sprinkle enough ultra-thick embossing powder over the card to cover it, tap off the excess and then heat to melt the powder with a heat gun. Repeat, inking up the embossed surface with more embossing ink. Sprinkle on more powder and heat to melt again.

Remove Stamp When Cool

While the resin is still warm, press into it with a large rubber stamp that is inked with a solid color to contrast with the painted background. (Here I used black.) Allow the card to cool with the stamp on it, then gently peel the card away from the stamp.

I exist as I am,

that is enough. Walt Whitman.

VIEW LIFE

Chrissy Howes

Chrissy Howes

Stacie Rife

Tonia Davenport

Tonia Davenport

Tonia Davenport

Tonia Davenport

DIMENSIONAL RESIN

If you love secret, buried treasure, this is the process for you. For the card demonstrated here, I went a step further and cast a resin face from the same material used to make the card, but you can have just as much fun without the extra effort. The back of the cooled card is stamped for even more dimension, and just about anything can be encased in the hot resin, provided it won't melt or run. Fibers, paper, charms . . . all fair game.

What You Will Need

ultra-thick embossing
   powder (Ranger)

hot pot

silicone mold

scissors

mica

metal repair tape

embossing ink

heat gun

assorted embellishments

baby wipes

rubber stamp

Pour Resin into Mold

Melt some resin in a hot pot, then pour it into a silicone mold.
The one here is of a face.

Cut Mica into Card Shape

To create a card form out of mica and metal repair tape, first cut
out a card shape from the mica with scissors.

Form Walls with Tape

Cut a strip of tape the width of the card and position the tape about
¼" (6mm) onto the edge of the mica. Roll the tape down to create
a semi-sturdy wall.

Fill Card Form with Resin

Repeat for the other three sides of the card, adding additional tape around the corners for a good seal. Coat the inside of the mold with embossing ink, coating the mica and the inside walls of the tape. Pour enough ultra-thick embossing powder into the mold to fill it about halfway. Tilt the form to spread the melted substance evenly around. Heat the resin with the heat gun to aid in the spreading.

Add Embellishments

Set embellishments into the warm, sticky resin, then pour in enough new ultra-thick embossing powder to fill the mold. Allow to cool.

Top with Final Elements

Press final embellishments into the top and set it aside to cool.

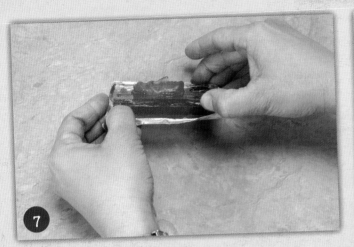

Clean Card

Peel the cooled card out of the mold. Ta-da! Clean off the finished card with a baby wipe.

Stamp on Back

To finish, stamp the back of the card with a rubber stamp. Ink up the stamp, lay it faceup on the table, then set the card onto it.

Stacie Rife

NO-sew faBRIC

Fabric can replace paper in many applications, and this includes artist trading cards. But don't think that means you have to own or use a sewing machine. An iron and fusible webbing make it easy to adhere fabric pieces of any size or shape to a card, or to other pieces of fabric. After the fabric is fused (whether as a background or smaller pieces as accents), it can be hand-stitched, painted or embellished in any other way, just like paper.

What You Will Need

carbon paper

muslin

image to trace (black-
  and-white works best)

stylus

Copic markers

fabric pastels (Pastel
  Dye Sticks–Pentel)

scrap paper

iron

fusible webbing

felt

scissors

BELOVED

Rebecca Zuniga

Corinne Stubson

Transfer Image to Muslin

Set a piece of carbon paper between the muslin and the image to trace, then go over all predominant lines with a pencil or stylus.

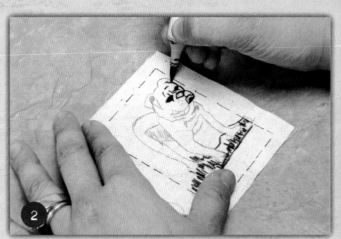

Retrace Lines with Marker

Go over the carbon lines with a Copic marker.

Apply Color with Pastels

Color in the image and the background with fabric pastels.

Heat–Set Pastel Color

Place a scrap of paper over the colored muslin and heat-set it with an iron.

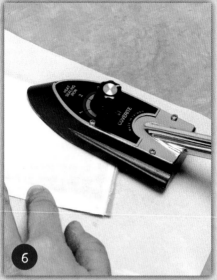

Add Details with Markers

Add final color and details with Copic markers.

Fuse Muslin to Felt

Cut a piece of fusible webbing slightly larger than the size of the muslin "card" and, using the iron, fuse it to a piece of felt. Peel off the backing and then use the backing as a protective layer to iron the colored muslin to the felt.

Trim Excess Felt

Trim the excess felt with scissors to finish.

Lesley Riley

Anna Barrow-Boekweg

Gloria Page

Stacie Rife

Maija Lepore

Reiny Rizzi

Reiny Rizzi

1+2=3

FUSED FIBERS

This technique gives your cards a very unique and intriguing texture by incorporating an iron, assorted decorative fibers, fusible webbing and embossing powder. I just think it's fun to melt things together, don't you? Sometimes the resulting patterns of the fibers will look great for a card as is, but if you prefer this effect as a background, it's easy to glue or attach elements over it.

What You Will Need

- fusible webbing (roll or sheet form)
- yarn or decorative fibers
- assorted embossing powders
- silicone craft sheet
- iron
- scissors

Set Web on Card
Lay fusible webbing over your blank card.

Create a Nest of Fibers
Make a little nest on top of your card with assorted fibers of your choice and a bit more fusible webbing.

Sprinkle Powder over Fibers
Randomly sprinkle assorted embossing powders over the nest.

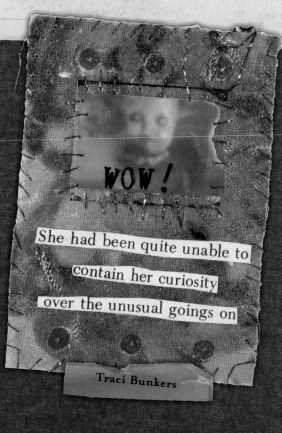

WOW!

She had been quite unable to contain her curiosity over the unusual goings on

Traci Bunkers

Heat with Iron

Gently place a heat-resistant craft sheet over the card and its nest, and apply heat over the entire surface, pressing it with an iron. After you have applied heat to the top, turn the card over and apply heat to the back of the card with the iron.

Cool and Peel

Let the card cool and then gently peel off the craft sheet.

Trim Excess Fibers

Use scissors to trim the excess fiber and webbing around the card.

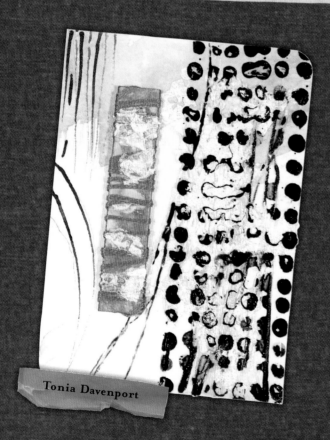

Tonia Davenport

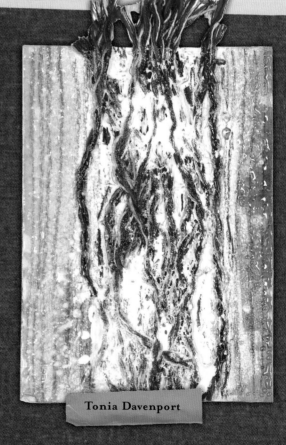

Tonia Davenport

beautiful

Marie Otero

Suzette McGrath

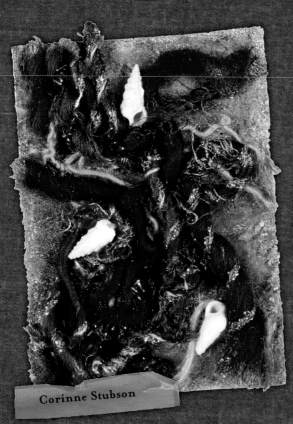

Corinne Stubson

PURE

Tonia Davenport

HAND-STITCHING

There's something so personal and inviting about a piece that's been hand-stitched. While it's fun to add stitching to cards that are made of fabric and produce a quilted look, you can also add hand-stitching to paper or painted cards for added texture. Embroidery thread comes in hundreds of colors and seems to work the best for adding a hand-touched element to cards, but try stitching in other fibers as well, such as string, yarn, raffia or even dental floss.

What You Will Need

patterned fabric
ATC Wizard (or paper template)
pencil
scissors
needles
stuffing
sewing thread
assorted colors of embroidery floss
muslin
color photocopy image to transfer
gel medium
sanding block (optional)
assorted embellishments

Jen Osborn

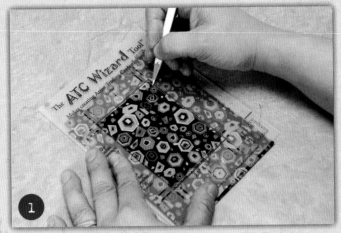

Trace Card Shape

Fold the fabric in half and trace over the area you want to use with the template. I used a white pencil here so I could see it.

Baste-Stitch Three Sides

Cut out the card shape, about 1/8" (3mm) outside of the pencil line. Baste-stitch three sides along the pencil line. Don't worry about it being perfect.

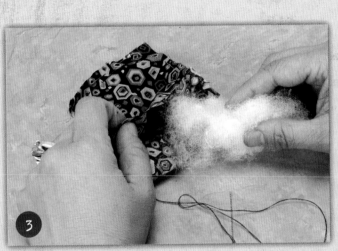

Add Stuffing

Stuff the card with just a small amount of batting.

Whip-Stitch All Sides

Sew the final side closed. Thread a length of embroidery floss through a needle and fold the fabric over along the pencil line and whip-stitch it down around the entire card. You may remove the basting stitches if they are still visible.

5

Add Quilting Stitches

With a new color of thread, add several quilting stitches. These can be random.

6

Apply Gel Medium Transfer

Make a transfer onto a piece of muslin, using gel medium (see page 45).

7

Sew on Transfer and Buttons

Trim the transfer down, leaving a bit of muslin outside of the image to fray the edges a bit. If you like, you can distress the image by sanding it with a sanding block. Sew the transfer to the card, using a third color of thread and a basting stitch. Finally, add a few embellishments such as buttons.

In Crochet

2: Turn work, sl st to tip o cluster, * ch 4, 3 tr cluster ove ch 2 of previous row with a c ween (total of 5 tr cluster), ch n top of next 2 tr cluster, rep

Nancy Breen

Angela Cartwright

Jen Osborn

Angela Cartwright

Maureen Blackman

Rebecca Zuniga

Lesley Riley

Christine Doyle

follow your

MACHINE SEWING

Not only is sewing with a sewing machine one of the strongest ways to secure layers together, it's also hard to beat for instant gratification! (Oh, and it looks cool, too!) Straight-stitching is, of course, the most common, but other stitches like zigzag and decorative embroidery can also be made with many of today's machines. You may find you need a sturdy needle in your machine if you're going to be sewing through dense layers like heavy fabric, cardstock and paper.

What You Will Need

fabric
sewing machine
paper element
needles
embroidery floss
page from a book
transparency
photo
gel medium
ink pad

ON FaBRIC

Zigzag Around the Card

Cut out a piece of fabric that is just a little bit larger than the card. With the fabric facedown and the card on top of it, sew a zigzag stitch around the perimeter of the card. Feel free to be loose with the line.

Sew on Paper Element

Fray the edges of the fabric a bit. On the top of the card, sew on a paper element, such as this heart-shaped image.

Add Hand-Stitches

Finish off with some hand-sewn decorative stitches, using embroidery floss.

ON PaPER

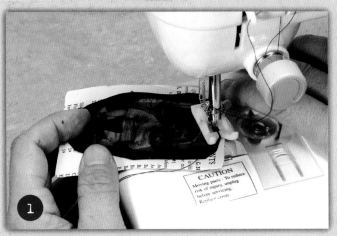

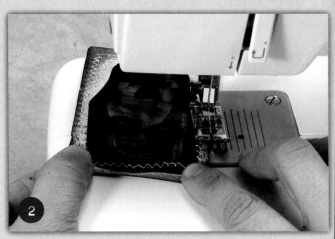

Secure Papers and Sew

Sew together a book page (trimmed to the card size), part of a photo and a transparency. You may wish to secure the elements with gel medium to prevent shifting as you sew.

Add Decorative Stitching

Add some color around the edges with an ink pad, then add a zigzag stitch around the outside edge, or around a certain part of the image you want to highlight.

Zoe Enright

Stephanie Neumann

a woman of spirit and capacit

Kathy Ingmundson

WILLIAM H

Carol Funicelli

Corey Moortgat

recognition.

Judi Pepin

bliss

happy

HEART'S DESIRE

Anna Barrow-Boekweg

Tracie Lampe

PRINCESS

Tracie Lampe

They began to whisper

that this beautiful maiden was probably
a witch who had dazzled their eyes and

put a spell on the king

Traci Bunkers

METAL TAPE

Many cool art supplies are found at your local hardware store, and metal repair tape is no exception. While its original purpose is to repair duct work, it works extremely well as a mixed-media foundation. It's very flexible and easy to emboss. It can also be given beautiful, vibrant color with alcohol inks. If you love the look of metal, but don't wish to dapple in the hard-core stuff, you're going to love working with this tape.

What You Will Need

metal repair tape
alcohol inks
blending solution
   (Ranger)
heat gun
brayer
scissors
rubber stamp
ink pad
stylus
brush
black fluid
   acrylic paint
paper towels

Add Solution to Inks

Add several droplets of the inks to a strip of the metal tape. Then add a few drops of the blending solution.

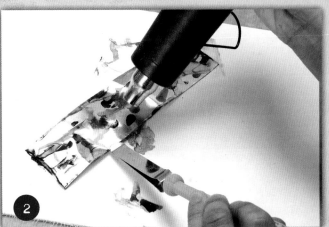

Heat and Spread Inks

Use a heat gun to blow around the droplets and the solution. Continue adding more ink and solution as desired until you have the look you want.

Tear Tape into Pieces

When the tape has cooled enough that you can handle it, tear the tape into several small pieces.

Brayer Pieces to Card

Layer the pieces onto the card, brayering as you go.

Emboss with Stylus

Additional pieces of tape that have been cut into shapes can be stamped on and then embossed with a stylus.

Add Black Paint

After embossing, brush over the embossed piece with black paint, taking care to work the paint into all of the crevices. Then, buff off the paint with a paper towel.

Add Additional Shapes

If you'd like, you can go back and add a bit of paint to the edges of the embossed piece to help it stand out from the background. Color some shapes in solid with the alcohol inks, like these hearts, and then layer the pieces onto the card.

The

glamor

Marie Otero

Josie Cirincione

Gloria Page

Stacie Rife

Douceur, mildness.

Céline Navarro

MICa

For me, mica equals magic. This transparent, natural material comes packaged in sheet form. It can be separated into plies of various thicknesses, and the thinner the ply, the less apparent the color in the mica. (It's naturally a sepia tone.) Even in very thin layers, mica is surprisingly sturdy, and it's the perfect material for making a sandwich! While anything thin can go between two layers, I love inserting a transparency image and a bit of alcohol ink between the mica pieces for a card you can see all the way through.

What You Will Need

protective surface

mica

scissors

alcohol inks

ink extender/blending
    solution (Ranger)

heat gun

transparency

gel medium

item, such as a
    pressed flower

1/8" (3mm)
    hole punch

1/8" (3mm) eyelets

eyelet setting tool

pixy (pik'si), *n.* a mischievous fairy.

Split Mica

Split a large piece of mica into a couple of thinner layers.

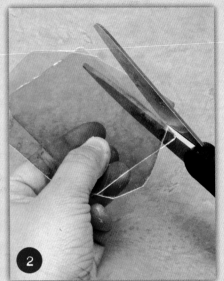

Trim to Card Size

Trim it down with scissors, using a card as a template.

Add Inks and Spread

Drop bits of alcohol inks onto the mica. Add some ink extender to spread the inks around. Sometimes I use a heat gun to spread the ink, as well.

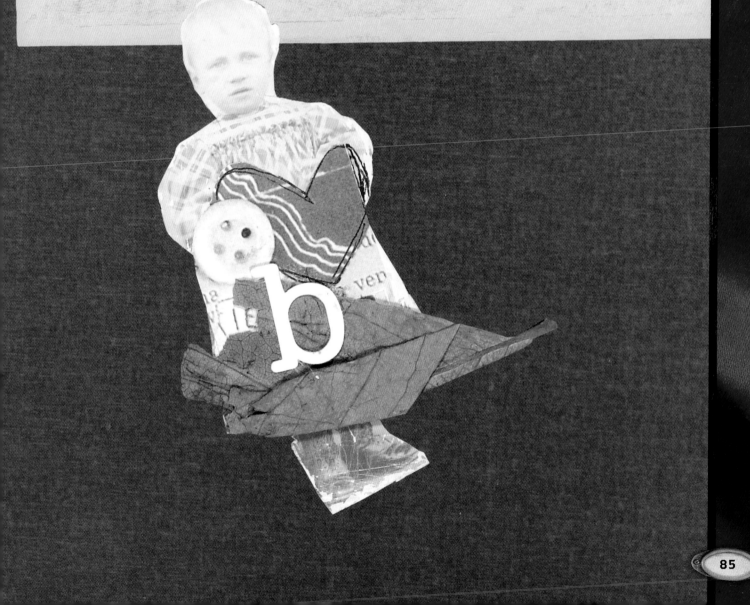

View Transparency

After the ink on the mica is dry, try out your transparency behind the inked mica. If there is too much ink that will be over an area of the image that you don't want covered or colored, you can go back and add more blending solution to dilute it or make it disappear.

Secure Items and Punch Holes

Dab a bit of gel medium around the outside of the transparency and to the pressed flower (or other item of your choice), and adhere it to the back piece of mica. Punch holes in the corners of the mica sandwich with the hole punch.

Set Eyelets

Set the eyelets in the corner to secure the sandwich together.

Chrissy Howes

Nancy Breen

together

13

Sarah Fishburn

the secret

Maija Lepore

Ah! le coquin!

il pleure

Céline Navarro

FRIENDLY PLASTIC

Friendly Plastic is a moldable plastic that is sold either as individual sticks or by the pound. It comes in a large array of solid colors and patterns. It's fun to cut up pieces and arrange them like a mosaic, using a paper card as a template. When warmed, the plastic is fused together and can also be trimmed down if necessary. My favorite thing to do with this cool medium is to stamp into it while it's warm with a rubber stamp and pigment ink. The finished piece looks like it was time-consuming, but it's really not at all. Try it!

What You Will Need

Friendly Plastic

Teflon or other heat-resistant sheet

scissors

blank ATC (to use as a template)

heat gun

stamp (optional)

pigment ink pad (optional)

decorative eyelets (optional)

leafing pen (Krylon)

Arrange Strips on Card

Working on a Teflon craft sheet, cut the plastic into pieces and tile them together on a card template.

Fuse Together

Use a heat gun to heat the plastic and fuse the pieces together. This takes a couple of minutes, so be patient.

Fill in Gaps

If you have gaps, you can fill them in with small pieces of the plastic, then reheat.

Trim Excess Plastic

Let the plastic cool enough that you can handle it, then trim off the excess plastic, if you have any, using scissors. As the plastic is cooling, it may try to curl in on itself. Just keep bending it flat.

Stamp While Warm

If you wish, you can now reheat the plastic, then stamp into it with stamps that have been inked with juicy pigment ink. Leave the stamp in the plastic until it cools; then the stamp will release easily. (You may need to reheat and flatten again after each stamping.) I also like to push eyelets into the warm plastic as a final touch.

EL CORAZON

Rebecca Zuniga

NIGHT IS A
STEALTHY EVIL RAVEN
WRAPT TO THE EYES
IN HIS BLACK WINGS
TB ALDRICH

ultra-cards

THE CARDS YOU'LL SEE IN THIS SECTION ARE THE SUPERSTARS OF ATCs—cards that go the extra mile and allow the creator to stretch his creative muscle. That doesn't mean they are difficult or for advanced artists only. They just might be the types of cards that you wouldn't expect to see.

Feel free to use what you learned from the last section to complete these cards. Consider this the perfect opportunity to combine techniques and mix and match them to really put your own spin on things.

JOURNaLeD CarDs

I have always loved journals and have longed to find the time to make an art journal. If you're like me, consider this an easy way to get a taste of journaling—with little commitment! And, if you are already keeping an art journal, consider scanning some of your favorite pages, reducing them, and making color copies to mount on trading cards. If you plan on trading your journaled cards, you don't need to share your innermost secrets . . .unless you want to!

Tawnya Romig-Foster

Tawnya Romig-Foster

Sometimes I wonder what great thing I'd be if I didn't have to stop BEING ME to make someone else happy.

Linda Woods

I spend too much time worried about loose screws.

Linda Woods

Lost on the way, as usual
Antique pins and the crazy lady
We snuck in the old school house

Our Cold Mountain

Karen Dinino

The storm is in my head

Karen Dinino

FOLDED CARDS

Folded cards can be any shape or size when unfolded, but they are usually folded to be the standard card size. Folds can add a whole new dimension and create limitless possibilities. This will stretch you creatively and make you think outside the box!

Corinne Stubson

Corinne Stubson

Kelly Snelling

Maija Lepore

Kim Rae Nugent

Suzette McGrath

DIPTYCH + TRIPTYCH CARDS

A diptych is a painting or work of art made of two parts, while a *triptych* is a painting or work of art consisting of three panels. One presentation possibility is to hinge the cards so they can be closed like a book to protect the interior paintings. Shrines, gold and sacred things come to mind when I think of diptych and triptych cards, but there really are no limits to the style of art that would suit this design solution.

Corinne Clark

Greg Nock

Terry Sullivan

Lynne Perrella

PEN + INK CARDS

The use of pen and ink is perfect for this small format. Think of all the times you've doodled on a small pad while talking on the phone—now try it on a trading card! Whether you prefer the simplicity of black and white or you really like to play with color, the definition of pen and ink can add a sophistication to your cards in a way that few other mediums can.

Anne Bagby

Anne Bagby

Anne Bagby

Anne Bagby

Anne Bagby

Digital Cards

Digital cards are amazing things to collect. If you are new to the world of computer-aided art, a very nice program that is easier to use than the professional Adobe Photoshop is Adobe Photoshop Elements.

Denise Tedeschi

Denise Tedeschi

Denise Tedeschi

leave

a message

Linda Woods

namaste

Linda Woods

home

Marie Otero

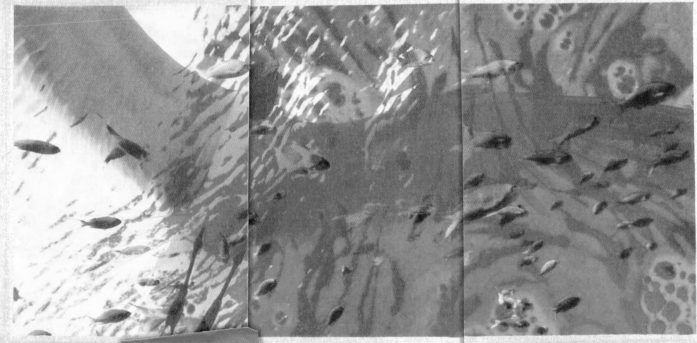

Cards for Children

Think of how much more art you'll be able to put on the refrigerator if your kids make artist trading cards. Their size is great for storing, mailing and, of course, swapping with other kids' cards. They can also be educational—as artistic versions of traditional flash cards. Schoolwork will be more fun for your kids if they can make art and do research for their studies at the same time! They can learn from the cards, and then swap them when they're done.

Brent Dinino

WISHING

You . . . .

Emily Dinino

•NOVEMBER 200 • 6 yrs old •

I see the 🍎

BY Finn

Finn Foster

WILD

Emily Dinino

Dear Diary,

"Say what's on your mind"

Emily Dinino

The top was too high for me to see.

Emily Dinino

monsters are not real. I don't believe in monster

Brent Dinino

WEESNAW
THE WORD THAT
MEANS EVERYTHING!!!

Brent Dinino

I just ate Cheetos.

Can you tell?

Emily Dinino

103

storage for artist trading cards

NOW THAT YOU'VE SEEN MANY CREATIVE TECHNIQUES for making artist trading cards, you're probably already busy creating a stash of your own that you'll be anxious to trade with others. Or you may become so attached to them that you'll want to keep many for yourself. Either way, you're going to need a nice place to store your cards.

I have amassed hundreds of cards, and I store most of them in three-ring binders, in sleeves that are designed especially for trading cards. This makes it easy for me to organize them and to view many at one time.

But sometimes I prefer to put a special group of cards in a book or container that gives them just a little extra status. The recycled can, the altered tin and the accordion book that I'll share with you on the following pages are examples of these special containers. These showcase solutions are great for housing cards that you've gotten from a collaborative swap with a particular theme or that you've accumulated from a particular memorable trading event. They would also make great gifts for friends who you'd like to introduce to your trading world!

"I am what I am."

aCCORDION BOOK

The secret to this colorful, folded booklet is to stamp with bleach on black cardstock. A variety of texture and form comes from using several stamps, and spray webbing is the icing on the cake! Just have fun with this project; don't think too hard about it. This booklet will hold twelve cards (six on each side), but you could make it longer with additional cardstock.

What You Will Need

black cardstock

paper towels

disposable Styrofoam plate

bleach

stamps

sponges

dye ink pads

Lumiere paints

stencil

spray webbing, two colors

$1/2$" (12mm) ribbon, about 2' (61cm)

double-stick tape

plastic trading card sleeves

dyed tissue paper

gel medium

Stamp with Bleach

Fold up a paper towel and set it in a Styrofoam plate. Pour several tablespoons of bleach over the paper towel. Use the damp towel as a pad for the stamps, and stamp bleach over the surface of the card.

Color Bleached Areas

Working with a separate sponge for each dye ink pad, color in the bleached areas with random bits of color.

Pounce on Luminescent Paint

Continue adding color to the entire card. Then, use a stencil and a sponge to pounce on the Lumiere paint.

Add Spray Webbing

Finally, add a bit of spray webbing.

Stamp Ribbon

Stamp along the entire length of the ribbon to tone down the brightness a bit.

Secure Ribbon

Secure the ribbon to the first panel with double-stick tape.

Adhere Sleeves

Adhere one plastic card protector to the first panel of the book, over the ribbon, with double-stick tape. Tear or cut the tissue paper into small strips (about ½" [12mm] wide) and adhere them over the edges of the bottom and sides of the plastic sleeve with gel medium. Repeat on each panel.

Gail Russakov

Marie Otero

altered square tin

The can you see here started as a tin for collecting fantasy/science fiction cards, so its size was perfect, but you could just as easily use a standard Band-Aid can for this project. Sanding the can before altering it gives the metal some tooth, and you will find the gesso and inks adhere better to it when it's no longer glossy with the original paint. While I've used a general design here that could work for any group of cards, you might decide to give your tin a theme to reflect a specific group of cards you want to store inside.

What You Will Need

trading card can

sanding block

brush

gesso

palette paper

alcohol inks

blending solution
   (Ranger)

permanent dye ink pad

heat gun

stamps

Sand off Paint

Using a sanding block, remove the majority of the paint that is printed on the can, but leave traces of it here and there.

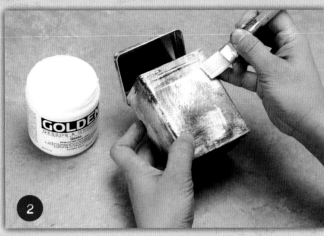

Apply Gesso

When you are happy with the amount of paint remaining, wipe the tin down to remove paint dust, then drybrush some of the areas with gesso. Let dry.

Add Inks

Working over a piece of palette paper, randomly drop assorted colors of ink onto the can surface and include some blending solution here and there. Facilitate moving the ink and drying with the heat gun. The can may get hot, so handle it carefully.

Stamp Randomly

If some areas of the can come out too dark, drybrush over them with a bit more gesso. Stamp randomly over the dried inks with stamps of your choice.

RECYCLED TIN CAN

I love when I can recycle items and do responsible things for the environment. Making an ATC vessel from the can you were going to throw away after eating soup for lunch is one way to do just that. If you don't like the look of rust that I created here, you could gesso and paint the can or experiment with a patina solution instead. In any case, you will need to use the type of can opener that cuts the rim off of the can (rather than just the portion inside of the rim); otherwise, the lid will fall into the can.

What You Will Need

tin can
can opener (Good Cook)
hex nut
screw
bolt
washer
epoxy (Liquid Nails)
brush
rusting solution
  (Modern Options:
  "Instant Rust-set")
pages with text from an
  old book
gel medium
metal repair tape
stylus
black paint
paper towels
acrylic paints in rusty
  colors

Adhere Hardware

Use a special type of can opener that leaves no sharp edges to remove the tin can top. Glue hex nuts to the bottom for feet, then assemble the bolt and the screw together, using epoxy to hold them. Put them in the washer and glue that onto the lid. Don't worry about the epoxy seeping because it will look like solder after the rust is applied.

Apply Iron Paint

Once the epoxy has dried (at least an hour—it takes twenty-four hours to cure), paint the can and lid with the instant iron paint. Let it dry. (This may take up to twenty-four hours.)

Brush on Rusting Solution

Apply the instant rusting solution next, brushing it on and then letting it dry.

Adhere Book Text

Tear up some old book pages and adhere several pieces around the can with gel medium.

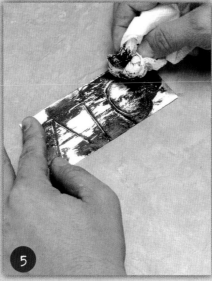

Create Metal-Tape Label

To make a label for the can, start with a piece of metal repair tape, about 2" x 5" (5cm x 13cm), and using a stylus, emboss "ATCs" on it, freehand. Apply some black paint over the embossing, and then wipe off the paint with a paper towel. Affix the metal tape label to the can.

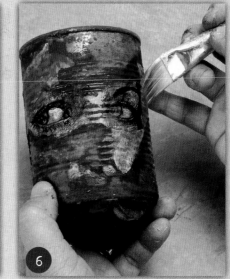

Paint Paper Elements

Apply a wash of rusty-colored acrylic over the text and image pieces to tie them in with the rust on the can. Wash over the metal tape as well.

collect + swap

By now you have seen many techniques that can be applied to these wonderful minature works of art. So what do you do with all of the great cards you make? I know I don't need to tell you by now, but just in case you've forgotten: You trade them!

Ideally, cards are traded in person. Because the philosophy behind ATCs is to connect with other artists, this can be most rewarding when you meet someone face-to-face. Trading sessions often take place at local stamp stores or art supply stores, or even in the homes of individuals belonging to a particular art group. Many stamp stores post events on a community bulletin board or in a company newsletter, so check with a store near you. Trading is also popular at national art retreats and conventions.

While trading sessions that provide in-person swapping are the nicest ways to meet other artists, sometimes they just aren't feasible or practical. As you're probably guessing, that is where the Internet comes in. It's easier now than ever before to connect with other artists online. Yahoo! Groups and LiveJournal are just two places among many to find forums and groups of individuals to trade with. Online, it's easy to join an existing collaborative swap or start your own. Cards can be traded as originals, as one (or more) in an edition or as part of a series.

Original cards are, of course, one-of-a-kind pieces of art. While there are no restrictions to the media used, sometimes there are restrictions put on cards at specific trading sessions that mandate that each card fit in a plastic sleeve. Other groups enjoy creating and collecting cards with a lot of depth to them, such as those with added embellishments or many layers.

Cards that are part of an edition are among several cards that have been either created to look alike or copied on a copier and then mounted onto cardstock. These cards should be numbered on the back as $\frac{1}{8}$ (the first of eight cards in this edition), $\frac{2}{8}$, $\frac{3}{8}$ and so on.

A series of cards includes different designs that pertain to a particular theme. These are popular with online groups, and you will find there are as many different themes as there are tastes.

As you probably noted on pages 104–113, there are clever and creative options for storing your cards, as well as more practical ways, such as a three-ring binder filled with trading card sleeves. I find my vast collection of cards to be not only something to help me reflect on all of the great people I have met through the years, but also a huge source of inspiration whenever I am experiencing a temporary art-making slump.

See the following pages for more information on signing cards (a very important part of the process). I hope I have inspired you to start creating and swapping cards right away if you aren't doing so already. Be sure to check out the gallery section that follows. You'll be astounded by some of the great works there. I hope we get the opportunity to trade with one another in the future. Happy creating, collecting and swapping!

SWAPPING CARDS ONLINE

The following groups can be found at Yahoo! Groups and are a great alternative to in-person trading sessions.

http://groups.yahoo.com/group/artisttradingcards/
http://groups.yahoo.com/group/ATC_World/
http://groups.yahoo.com/group/ArtTradingCards/
http://groups.yahoo.com/group/ArtErratica/
http://groups.yahoo.com/group/Collagecats/
http://groups.yahoo.com/group/Bmuse/
http://groups.yahoo.com/group/clothpaperstudio/
http://groups.yahoo.com/group/Habiliments/

GALLERY OF SIGNATURES

Including your signature on the backs of your cards is an important step and one that should never be omitted. Remember, when you trade a card with someone, you are sharing a part of yourself. The recipient of your card will want to be able to refer to who gave her the card weeks, months or years down the road.

Some artists really get into this aspect of the cards and create self-portrait signature cards that they print in mass quantity, making it easy to slap one on the back of each card created. In fact, sometimes the signature on the back of the card can be as elaborate as the artwork on the front!

Information to include on the back is optional, but the most common things to include are: title of the work, date, edition number (if applicable), contact information (such as an e-mail address) and of course, your name! I will often make up a new signature card for each new series I participate in. This part of the process can be as simple or as involved as you would like it to be.

Anna Barrow-Boekweg

diptych
fiber
layers
machine sewing

tawnyaromigfoster@hotmail.com

Tawnya Romig-Foster

TRACI BUNKERS

P.O. BOX 442099
LAWRENCE, KS 66044
HTTP://WWW.BONKERSFIBER.COM

Traci Bunkers

BERNIE BERLIN

Bernie Berlin

Thecre8tivei@aol.com

WWW.PICTURETRAIL.COM/THECRE8TIVEI

Giuseppina Cirincione

Phoenix, AZ 85013

Josie Cirincione

WINGGLEAM 002
handcrafted by
SUZETTE MCGRATH
WINGGLEAM.CO.UK

Suzette McGrath

tRacie LaMpe

Tracie Lampe

www.silverfishes.com
p.o. box 160, center hill, fl 33514

maria_lamb@silverfishes.com

TITLE: OUR AUNT BETTY

Hillsborough River State Park

Sarah Fishburn

BERNIE BERLIN

Thecre8tivei@aol.com

Bernie Berlin

Patricia Anders

Patricia Anders

Patricia Anders

Katie Kendrick

Tracie Lampe

Molly

Whuppie

Maria Lamb

Kelly Snelling

Kelly Snelling

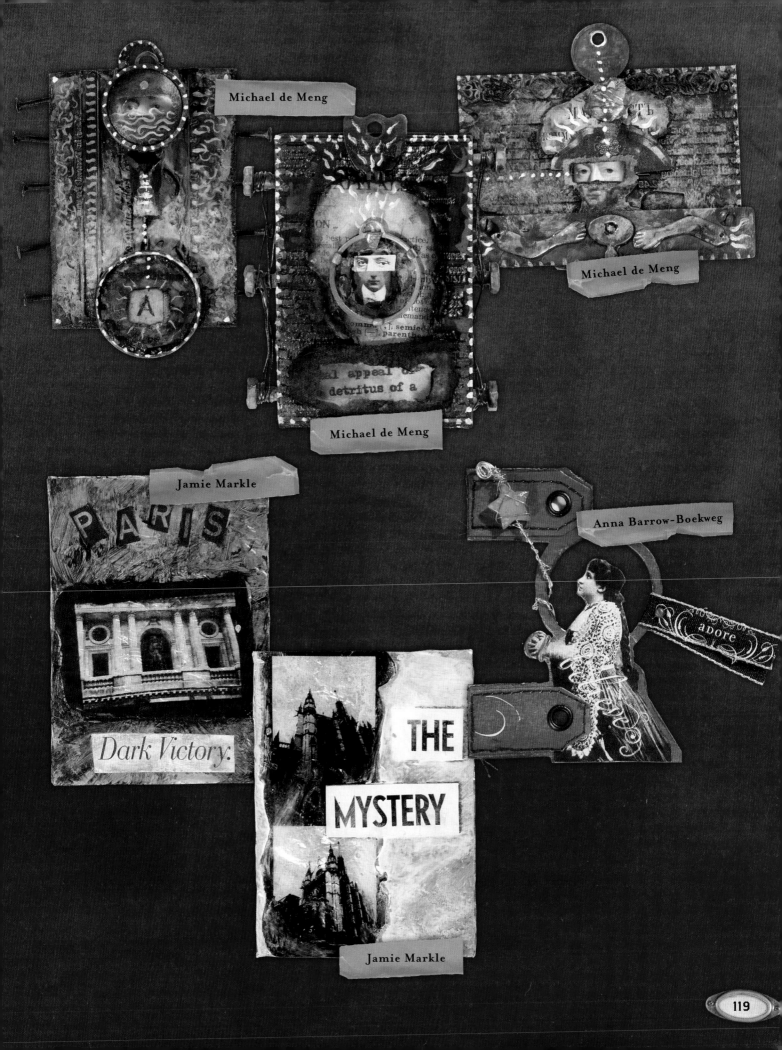

Michael de Meng

Michael de Meng

Michael de Meng

Jamie Markle

PARIS

Dark Victory.

THE MYSTERY

Jamie Markle

Anna Barrow-Boekweg

adore

Carla Naron

Nº 10-98-19

Chrissy Howes

bloom

Carla Naron

Colette George

Corinne Clark

Colette George

Go fiSH

Christine Doyle

fusion

Heather Crossley

behind

Lyn Cardinal

kiss

Jen Osborn

TRUE

PLEASE WRITE ALL THE REALLY IMPORTANT STUFF HERE

Jen Osborn

TWO MINUS ONE EQUALS NOTHING.

Bernie Berlin

Barbe Saint John

Sarah Fishburn

Be a little wildflo...

Sarah Fishburn

my

playful

heart

Maureen Blackman

navigate : inside channels

Katie Kendrick

POST CARD

The weak can never forgive.

Forgiveness is
the attribute of the strong.

Bernie Berlin

And now I see with eye serene

Mary Haldeman

Tawnya Romig-Foster

Mary Haldeman

Bernie Berlin

Lost time is never...

Izabella Pierce

Bernie Berlin

"THE QUESTION IS NOT WHETHER WE WILL DIE, BUT HOW WE WILL LIVE."

CONTRIBUTING ARTISTS

PATRICIA ANDERS
Calabasas, California, United States
patricia@artpropensity.com
www.artpropensity.com
118

ANNE BAGBY
Estill Springs, Tennessee, United States
www.annebagby.com
99

ANNA BARROW-BOEKWEG
Royal Leamington Spa, Warwickshire,
United Kingdom
anna@barrow.wanadoo.co.uk
www.justannax.typepad.com/eden
26, 66, 79, 116, 119

MAUREEN BLACKMAN
Albourne, West Sussex, United Kingdom
maureen.blackman@virgin.net
47, 75, 122

NANCY BREEN
Loveland, Ohio, United States
19, 74, 86

TRACI BUNKERS
Lawrence, Kansas, United States
bonkers@bonkersfiber.com
www.bonkersfiber.com
69, 79, 116

LYN CARDINAL
Somerville, Massachusetts, United States
lyncardinal@yahoo.com
www.lyncardinal.com
26, 40, 121

ANGELA CARTWRIGHT
Los Angeles, California, United States
www.acartwrightstudio.com
30, 31, 43, 74, 75

GIUSEPPINA "JOSIE" CIRINCIONE
Phoenix, Arizona, United States
collagelnf@cox.net
www.collagelostandfound.com
43, 46, 83, 117

CORINNE CLARK
Mississauga, Ontario, Canada
corinnefree@gmail.com
www.pinkyswearsisters.com
96, 120

HEATHER CROSSLEY
Stretton Heights, Brisbane, Australia
mkhc@powerup.com.au
27, 49, 121

TONIA DAVENPORT
Mason, Ohio, United States
www.frameitwithtonia.com
43, 59, 70, 71

MICHAEL DE MENG
Missoula, Montana, United States
www.michaeldemeng.com
119

BRENT DININO
Westlake Village, California, United States
102, 103

EMILY DININO
Westlake Village, California, United States
102, 103

KAREN DININO
Westlake Village, California, United States
www.visualchronicles.com
93

CHRISTINE DOYLE
Bellevue, Kentucky, United States
54, 75, 121

ZOE ENRIGHT
Cincinnati, Ohio, United States
z.e@fuse.net
78

SARAH FISHBURN
Fort Collins, Colorado, United States
sarah@sarahfishburn.com
www.sarahfishburn.com
15, 23, 27, 46, 52, 53, 87, 117, 122

FINN FOSTER
Lakewood, Colorado, United States
102

CAROL FUNICELLI
Cincinnati, Ohio, United States
78

COLETTE GEORGE
Riddle, Oregon, United States
cdesigns@pioneer-net.com
19, 120

DIANE GLOS
Cincinnati, Ohio, United States
47

MARY HALDEMAN
Long Beach, California, United States
mehaldeman@aol.com
www.picturetrail.com/maryhaldeman
23, 53, 123

CLAUDINE HELLMUTH
Orlando, Florida, United States
www.collageartist.com
13, 30, 36

PETER HOLLINGHURST
Haywards Heath, West Sussex, United Kingdom
peter@hollinghurst.org.uk
http://hybridartifacts.livejournal.com
29, 31, 36, 41

CHRISSY HOWES
Cloquet, Minnesota, United States
howes237@hotmail.com
www.chrissyhowes.typepad.com
58, 86, 120

KATHY INGMUNDSON
South Lebanon, Ohio, United States
kaiquilts@yahoo.com
78

KATIE KENDRICK
Belfair, Washington, United States
joyouslybecoming@earthlink.net
www.katiekendrick.com
13, 26, 27, 41, 118, 122

MARIA LAMB
Center Hill, Florida, United States
maria_lamb@silverfishes.com
30, 41, 46, 118

ResOURCes

a message

American Crafts
801-226-0747
www.americancrafts.com
Galaxy markers

Artchix Studio
www.artchixstudio.com
ATC envelopes, collage sheets and other supplies

BCW Supplies
800-433-4229
www.bcwsupplies.com
trading card sleeves

Clearsnap, Inc.
888-448-4862
www.clearsnap.com
clear embossing ink pads, clear embossing powder

Crayola
800-272-9652
www.crayola.com
Portfolio water-soluble oil pastels

The Cre8tive Eye
www.picturetrail.com/thecre8tivei
Collage sheets and image CDs

European Papers, Ltd.
614-316-3948
www.europeanpapers.com
ATC Wizard Tool, precut card packs

The George Basch Company, Inc.
www.nevrdull.com
Nevr-Dull Magic Wadding Polish

Golden Artist Colors, Inc.
800-959-6543
www.goldenpaints.com
colored glazing medium, gel medium, acrylic paints

Invoke Arts
www.invokearts.com
ATC background stamps

Jacquard Products
800-442-0455
www.jacquardproducts.com
Lumiere metallic paints

Krylon
800-457-9566
www.krylon.com
metallic leafing pens, spray webbing

Ranger Industries, Inc.
732-389-3535
www.rangerink.com
ultra-thick embossing enamel (UTEE), melting pots, blending solution, silicone molds, nonstick craft sheets, alcohol inks

Stampington & Company
The Shoppe at Somerset
www.stampington.com
ATC papers and albums

Stamp Oasis
www.stampoasis.com
Luna Lights metallic paints

Triangle Coatings, Inc.
510-614-3900
www.modernoptions.com
Modern Options rust solution

Tsukineko
800-769-6633
www.tsukineko.com
VersaFine pigment ink pads

Utrecht Art Supplies
800-223-9132
www.utrechtart.com
Primary Artist liquid watercolor

She had been quite unable t

contain her curiosity

over the unusual goings on

INDULGE YOUR CREATIVE SIDE WITH THESE INSPIRING TITLES FROM NORTH LIGHT CRAFT

by Josie Cirincione

Inside *Collage Lost and Found*, you'll learn how to find and use old photographs, memorabilia and ephemera to create collages with a saucy style and a story to tell. Using her own Sicilian background as an example, author Josie Cirincione shows you how to examine your own passions for inspiration, as well as tips on where to look and what to look for. Then you'll choose from 20 step-by-step projects that use basic collage, jewelry-making and image transfer techniques to make sassy projects to decorate with, wear and give away as gifts.

ISBN-10: 1-58180-787-2
ISBN-13: 978-1-58180-787-5
paperback   128 pages   33461

by Traci Bautista

Learn to collage using everything but the kitchen sink with this bright and playful book. Author Traci Bautista shows you there are no mistakes in making art. You can combine anything—from paper, fabric, paint and even paper towels to beads, metal, doodles and stitching to create unique art books, fabric journals and mixed-media paintings. The book includes detailed instructions for lots of innovative techniques, such as staining/dying paper towels, freestyle hand lettering, doodling, funky embroidery and crayon transfers. Then you'll learn how to turn your newfound techniques into dazzling projects.

ISBN-10: 1-58180-845-3
ISBN-13: 978-1-58180-845-2
paperback   128 pages   Z0024

by Linda & Opie O'Brien

Discover a nontraditional approach to the introduction of working with metal as you create 20 fun and funky projects. This is the whimsical side of metal that not only teaches you how to cut and join metal surfaces, but also allows you to explore ways to age and add texture to metal, conjure up beautiful patina finishes and uncover numerous types of metal such as copper, mesh, wire and recycled material. Whether you've worked with metal before or you're new to the medium, give your recycled tin cans a second glance and start crafting beautiful pieces with metal today.

ISBN-10: 1-58180-646-9
ISBN-13: 978-1-58180-646-5
paperback   128 pages   33235

by Linda Woods & Karen Dinino

Have you always wanted to dive into art journaling, but you're always stopped by what to put on the page? Finally, there is a book that comes to your rescue! *Visual Chronicles* is your no-fear guide to expressing your deepest self with words as art, and artful words. Friendly projects like the Personal Palette and the Mini Prompt Journal make starting easy. You'll also find inspiration for experimenting with colors, shapes, ephemera, communicating styles, symbols and more!

ISBN-10: 1-58180-770-8
ISBN-13: 978-1-58180-770-7
paperback   128 pages   33442

These and other fine North Light titles are available at your local craft retailer or bookstore or from online suppliers.